WASHINGTON

WASHINGTON

HELLO
U.S.A.

by E. S. Powell

Lerner Publications Company

1825 3623
A

You'll find this picture of wildflowers in Mount Rainier National Park at the beginning of every chapter. Wildflowers grow in the foothills of Mount Rainier, which can be seen in the background, and in other parts of the Cascade Mountains. During spring and summer, hikers in the Cascades enjoy the beautiful display of color.

Cover (left): Ferry crossing a channel near Spieden Island. Cover (right): Seattle skyline. Pages 2–3: Palouse Falls in southeastern Washington. Page 3: Seattle waterfront.

This book is available in two editions:
Library binding by Lerner Publications Company, a division of Lerner Publishing Group
Soft cover by First Avenue Editions, an imprint of Lerner Publishing Group
241 First Avenue North
Minneapolis, MN 55401 U.S.A.

Website address: www.lernerbooks.com

Library of Congress Cataloging-in-Publication Data

Powell, E. Sandy.
    Washington / by E. S. Powell (Revised and expanded 2nd edition)
       p.   cm. — (Hello U.S.A.)
    Includes index.
    ISBN: 0–8225–4053–3 (lib. bdg. : alk. paper)
    ISBN: 0–8225–4155–6 (pbk. : alk. paper)
       1. Washington (State)—Juvenile literature. [1. Washington (State)] I. Title.
    II. Series.
    F891.3.P69 2002
    979.7—dc21   2001000330

Manufactured in the United States of America
1 2 3 4 5 6 – JR – 07 06 05 04 03 02

CONTENTS

The Cascade Mountains *(above)* divide Washington into two very different areas—the evergreen west and the drier east *(opposite page)*.

THE LAND

The Evergreen State

Washington is well known for its evergreen pine and fir trees. In fact, its nickname is the Evergreen State. But only the lush western third of the state, from the Pacific coast to the Cascade Mountains, can truly be called evergreen. Most of Washington actually lies east of the Cascades. Here, rolling wheat fields and dry grasslands stretch mile after mile.

Bordering the Pacific Ocean in the northwestern corner of the United States, Washington belongs to the Pacific Northwest region of the country. Canada borders Washington on the north, and the state of Idaho lies to the east. To the south, the Columbia River creates much of the boundary between Oregon and Washington.

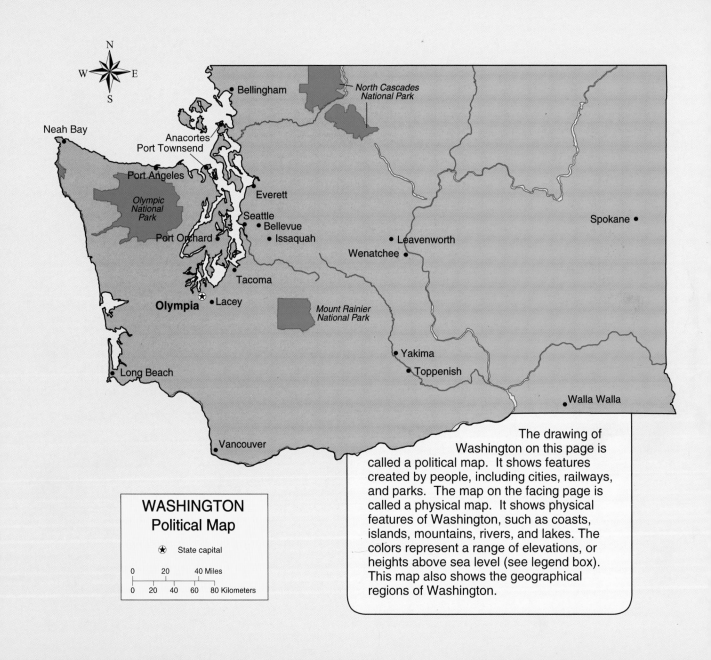

N **W** **E** **S**

Neah Bay

Bellingham

North Cascades
National Park

Anacortes
Port Townsend

Port Angeles

Olympic
National
Park

Everett

Seattle
Bellevue

Port Orchard

Issaquah

Leavenworth

Wenatchee

Spokane

Tacoma

Olympia • Lacey

Mount Rainier
National Park

Yakima

Toppenish

Long Beach

Walla Walla

Vancouver

WASHINGTON
Political Map

⭐ State capital

0   20   40 Miles

0 20 40 60 80 Kilometers

The drawing of
Washington on this page is
called a political map. It shows features
created by people, including cities, railways,
and parks. The map on the facing page is
called a physical map. It shows physical
features of Washington, such as coasts,
islands, mountains, rivers, and lakes. The
colors represent a range of elevations, or
heights above sea level (see legend box).
This map also shows the geographical
regions of Washington.

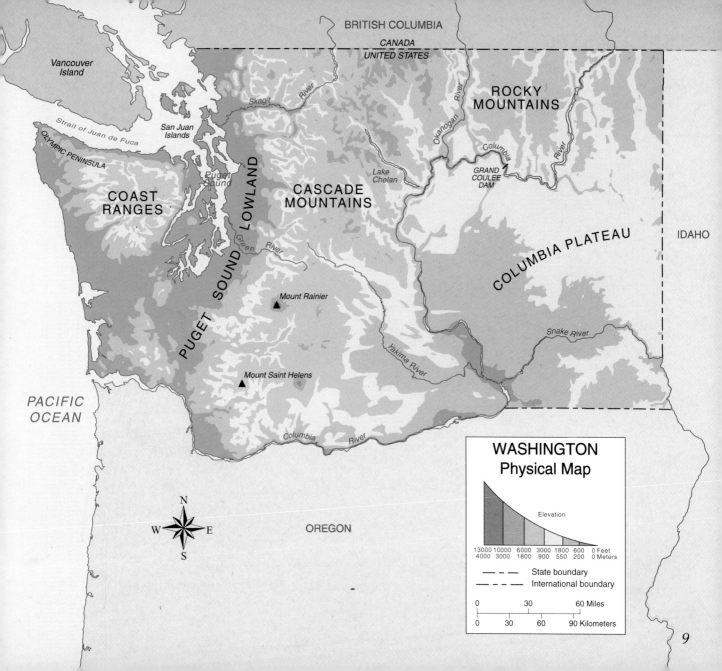

BRITISH COLUMBIA

CANADA
UNITED STATES

Vancouver
Island

ROCKY
MOUNTAINS

Skagit   River

Strait of Juan de Fuca

San Juan
Islands

Okanogan   River

Columbia   River

OLYMPIC PENINSULA

Puget
Sound

Lake
Chelan

GRAND
COULEE
DAM

COAST
RANGES

PUGET SOUND LOWLAND

CASCADE
MOUNTAINS

COLUMBIA PLATEAU

IDAHO

Green   River

Mount Rainier ▲

Snake River

Mount Saint Helens ▲

Yakima River

PACIFIC
OCEAN

Columbia   River

OREGON

N
W   E
S

WASHINGTON
Physical Map

Elevation

| 13000 | 10000 | 6000 | 3000 | 1800 | 600 | 0 Feet |
| 4000 | 3000 | 1800 | 900 | 550 | 200 | 0 Meters |

– – –   State boundary
– – – –   International boundary

| 0 | | 30 | | 60 Miles |
| 0 | 30 | 60 | | 90 Kilometers |

9

More than 300 million years ago, the western coast of North America was near what later became Idaho. Over time, several smaller continents moved through the Pacific Ocean, pushing into and joining the larger North American continent. The smaller landmasses formed the land that later became Washington. As the landmasses hit North America, they rumpled into the mountains we see along the coast.

Glaciers also helped shape Washington's varied landscape. When these huge sheets of ice melted, the sea level rose. Water from the Pacific Ocean poured into the low spots that the glaciers had carved out. This is how the Strait of Juan de Fuca was formed. A narrow water passageway, the **strait** separates northwestern Washington from Canada's Vancouver Island.

Water also flowed south from the eastern end of the strait, creating Puget Sound. The deep and sheltered waters of Puget Sound have made this long inlet an excellent place to dock large ships for loading and unloading goods.

Washington can be divided into five geographic regions—the Coast Ranges, the Puget Sound Lowland, the Cascade Mountains, the Columbia Plateau, and the Rocky Mountains. The mountains of the Coast Ranges line the Pacific Ocean. The rugged northern section of the Coast Ranges juts into the ocean and is known as the Olympic Peninsula. To the south, the mountains are much lower.

Inland, a long valley stretches north from Oregon, curves around Puget Sound, and goes all the way into Canada. Called the Puget Sound Lowland, this region is home to three out of four Washington residents.

Cape Flattery, the tip of the Olympic Peninsula, juts out into fog-covered waters.

The Puget Sound Lowland includes the San Juan Islands.

The scenic Cascade Mountains border the Puget Sound Lowland and rise as high as 14,410 feet at Mount Rainier. Several of the mountains in this range were once active volcanoes. Washington's largest natural lake, Lake Chelan, lies in the Cascades. It was actually once a river, but glaciers blocked the flow of the river with soil and rock, and the lake formed.

The wild beauty of the Cascade Mountains attracts Washingtonians with a taste for the outdoors.

East of the Cascade Mountains, glaciers also crossed the Columbia Plateau. When the glaciers started breaking up, they released huge floods of water that washed away the topsoil. This process left behind bare volcanic rocks called **scablands.** Only sagebrush and cheatgrass—plants that need little water and dirt—can grow in these areas. Gently rolling hills mark the **plateau,** a highland region.

This chilly snow cave *(above)* was created when glacial snow melted near the earth's surface. The Columbia Plateau *(right)* has many acres of golden wheat fields.

Northeastern Washington rises into the Rocky Mountain region. From this corner of the state flows the mighty Columbia River, which curves 700 miles through central Washington to the Pacific Ocean. The Okanogan River flows into the Columbia in northern Washington, and the Snake and Yakima Rivers join the Columbia in the south.

Northeastern Washington has two large rivers, the Columbia and the Okanogan *(above)*.

Countless rivers and streams pour west out of the Coast Ranges and the Cascades, providing plenty of water for plants and animals. Many of these waterways, among them the Skagit and the Green River, also supply water to the cities and towns of Puget Sound.

The climate in Washington depends on the location. West of the Cascades, the winters are mild. Summer days can top 90° F, with year-round rainfall around 60 inches. The Olympic Peninsula gets as much as 180 inches of rain per year, creating one of the few **rain forests** in the United States.

Abundant rain makes rain gear a must in many parts of western Washington.

Winter in eastern Washington is colder, with much more snow than western Washington. Summers can be very hot and dry. Average rainfall on the Columbia Plateau is only 6 inches per year.

In all, more than half of Washington is covered with forests of Douglas fir, Sitka spruce, western hemlock, red cedar, and pine. Western Washington's woods have thick undergrowth. Eastern Washington, with its sparse forests, has one particularly unusual tree— the western larch. Although this tree has cones like other evergreens, its needles turn orange and drop off each fall.

Colorful wildflowers contrast with many kinds of trees in Washington's countryside.

Sea lions *(right)* live along Washington's coast. Marmots *(below)* frolic on a grassy Cascades hillside.

The forests and lakes west of the Cascades provide homes for marmots, otters, beavers, and countless other animals. Deer and elk live throughout the state. Grouse and pheasant are plentiful in eastern Washington. Oysters grow on the rocky beaches. And whales can be spotted off the coast.

THE HISTORY

Natives and Newcomers

Long before Europeans came to what later became Washington, natural disasters struck the land. These disasters sometimes preserved clues that can help modern people understand ancient life. When Mount Saint Helens erupted about 3,500 years ago, the Indians, or Native Americans, who lived in the region must have fled. The only clues left about their life are ancient tools found buried under lava and ash.

Another big disaster happened sometime around A.D. 1500. Near Ozette on the Olympic Peninsula, a whole village was buried under a mud slide. When the village was discovered in 1970, buildings, skeletons, tools, sculptures, and baskets had all been perfectly preserved.

Native Americans carved these pictures on the rocks of the Olympic Peninsula before Ozette was buried in mud.

Because of the Ozette mud slide, we know that the Makah Indians dug clams and hunted whales with wooden spears that were 18 feet long. The sharp tips of the spears were made from mussel shells.

Other discoveries, as well as notes taken by the first white people to reach the area, have taught us about various groups of Indians in the Pacific Northwest. The way these tribes lived depended on whether they were west or east of the Cascade Mountains.

West of the Cascades, tribes such as the Nooksack, Snoqualmie, and Snohomish made use of the abundant cedar trees. The houses in their villages were made from cedar. They pounded cedar bark to be soft enough to make clothing. And they carved canoes out of cedar tree trunks.

Coastal Indian families sometimes gathered for a huge feast called a potlatch. Giving gifts was an important part of the celebration. The most honored chief gave away everything he owned.

The Makah Whalers

American Indians living along the Pacific coast depended on the sea for much of their food. But few groups undertook the life-threatening job of hunting whales. Among the daring were the Makah.

Whaling was a ritual for the Makah. To prepare for the hunt each spring, whalers and their wives fasted, bathed in hidden ponds, and recited secret prayers. Once a whale was spotted, the whalers would leave by canoe before dawn. Their wives stayed at home, lying perfectly still in the hopes that the whale would also be still.

The whaling crew paddled right up alongside the huge animal. Then the lead whaler would plunge his harpoon into the whale's shoulder. The harpoon had a barbed tip that anchored into the flesh, and a long line with sealskin floats was tied to the other end of the harpoon. The floats slowed the whale, so it could not swim as far away.

Meanwhile, the crew paddled quickly backward to get away, and they began to sing songs to encourage the whale to swim toward shore. As the whale dove downward, the men tied on more lines with floats to slow the creature even more.

By the time the whale surfaced, other men had arrived in canoes to help throw more harpoons into the animal. After it died, a crew member would jump overboard to tie the whale's mouth shut. This kept water out of the whale's stomach, so it wouldn't sink. The crew towed the huge carcass to shore, singing all the way. Villagers met them, welcoming the whale with songs and feasts.

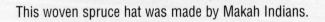

This woven spruce hat was made by Makah Indians.

Hanging fish on racks allowed them to dry in the sun. The dried fish could be easily stored for the winter.

For food, the western tribes caught salmon and other fish. They also gathered many edible plants from the dense forests, including the roots of cattails and wapatoo, parts from lupines, thistles, ferns, and many kinds of berries.

East of the mountains, the Yakima, Palouse, Spokane, and other groups lived along rivers. They traveled in spring and summer, searching for fresh fish, game, and berries. While these tribes were on the move, they set up portable lodges made from wood frames. Mats of woven grass were used to cover the frames. Travel became easier by about 1700, when the Palouse, Nez Percé, Cayuse, and others acquired horses by trading with tribes hundreds of miles to the south.

Indians of the Columbia Plateau used woven baskets to store bitterroot, which they first dried in the sun.

In the winter, eastern tribes dug pits to make houses that were partially underground. Sometimes the houses were built next to cliffs, which blocked harsh winds. Clothing made from deer, elk, and bighorn sheep skins kept people warm. They ate fried cakes made from pemmican. This mixture of dried meat, fish oil, and dried berries lasted through the winter without spoiling.

The Chinook, who lived near the Pacific Ocean along the mouth of the Columbia River, linked peoples west and east of the Cascades. They traveled upriver to trade shells and other valuable items with the families east of the mountains. For the most part, Native Americans in what later became Washington lived peacefully until white settlers began to arrive.

In the 1700s, Spanish, Russian, and British explorers sailed along the Pacific coast, making maps and trading with the coastal Indians. The Europeans bought the pelts of sea otters, beavers, and other animals. They then sold them for a huge profit in China, where the furs were popular.

It wasn't until 1792 that Captain Robert Gray from Boston sailed along the coast of the Pacific Northwest. He made it through the rough waters at the mouth of the Columbia and named the river after his ship.

The camas lily bulb looks like an onion and tastes somewhat like a sweet potato. These bulbs were a favorite food of Indians throughout Washington.

The Columbia River was named for explorer Robert Gray's ship, but the river had already been used for centuries by Native Americans on their way to trade with other tribes.

The Lewis and Clark expedition might never have reached the Pacific coast without the help of a Shoshone Indian woman named Sacagawea. She guided the American men and helped them communicate with the Native Americans they met.

That same year, George Vancouver from Great Britain explored the entire Washington coast and named several places—including Mount Baker, Mount Rainier, Puget Sound, and Whidbey Island—after his crew members. Vancouver also traveled up the Columbia and claimed the Pacific Northwest for Britain.

News of the Europeans' profitable fur trade reached the leaders of the United States. They paid two explorers, Meriwether Lewis and William Clark, to map a route from the Mississippi River to the Pacific Ocean.

Fort Vancouver served as a meeting place for Washington's early white settlers, who came there to trade goods.

The last section of the route was to follow the Columbia River. Lewis and Clark's route made it possible for American and British settlers to travel to the Pacific coast by land as well as by sea.

In 1825 John McLoughlin, a British Canadian, established a trading post on the Columbia River. Called Fort Vancouver, the post encouraged white settlers to come to the region. Some of the first to arrive were mountain men who lived alone all winter, trapping in the mountains and coming together once a year to trade.

Other early settlers came with the hope of bringing the Christian religion to the Indians. These settlers were known as **missionaries.** In 1836 the missionaries Marcus and Narcissa Whitman settled among the Cayuse Indians in southeastern Washington.

At first the Cayuse got along with the Whitmans and other white settlers in the area. But then there was a serious misunderstanding. The Whitmans had been sharing their vegetables with the Indians. One day, the Whitmans put poison around their garden to kill the mice that were eating the vegetables.

When some Cayuse caught the measles and died, the Indians thought the Whitmans had purposely poisoned them, too. So the chief had the Whitmans and several other whites killed. Trust between the two groups was broken, and the mission was destroyed.

The settlers brought several other diseases that were new to Native Americans and proved to be deadly. Cholera and smallpox took the lives of thousands of Indians.

Narcissa Whitman

Marcus Whitman

As more people from the eastern United States and Britain settled in the Pacific Northwest, the two countries agreed to divide the land. The British moved their fur trading operations north from Fort Vancouver to Vancouver Island in Canada. Under this agreement, the U.S. settlers would control the area known as the Oregon Territory.

In 1853 the Oregon Territory was divided into the Washington Territory and the Oregon Territory. The U.S. president appointed Isaac Stevens to be governor of Washington. Stevens convinced Indian tribes all over the territory to give up their claims to the land. In return he assigned them protected areas called **reservations,** where the Indians could live undisturbed by white settlers.

The written agreement between Stevens and the Indians, called a **treaty,** gave the Indians two years to move. When Stevens began moving whole villages immediately, the Native Americans fought back. But they had been so weakened by disease that they couldn't defend their land. The Yakima and other tribes were angry, discouraged, and sick

In this illustration, Isaac Stevens meets with Native American leaders in 1855 to negotiate a treaty.

at heart as they moved onto reservations and discovered that their lives would be completely different.

While Indians mourned the loss of their land and way of life, white settlers poured in from the east. The thick forests west of the Cascades provided what seemed like endless opportunities for lumberjacks. Sawmills worked furiously to make timber for building. Towns near the sawmills soon grew into cities, particularly around Puget Sound. From these cities near the Pacific, lumber could be shipped to California, Hawaii, and even Australia.

Some of the largest trees in the world were cut down in the early years of Washington's logging industry.

In the 1800s, fishers often caught salmon that weighed almost 100 pounds. During the next century, both the size and the number of fish declined.

Shipping became even more important in 1883, when the Northern Pacific Railway completed a cross-country line from the East Coast to Puget Sound. Some of the people who helped build the train tracks came from as far away as Asia.

By train, the journey between the East and West Coasts was much easier than by covered wagon. The trains brought many more settlers to the Washington Territory. Before long, it had enough people to apply for statehood, and in 1889 Washington became the 42nd state.

Besides lumber, the valleys west of the Cascades offered rich farmland, and fish were abundant. Life wasn't easy, though, since practically everything that people needed had to be homemade.

The Little Town That Could

Towns sometimes grow up around the dreams and enthusiasm of a single person. Spokane *(above)*, for instance, grew faster than any other city in Washington because of James Glover *(inset)*.

Determined to build a city he could call his own, Glover bought a sawmill in 1873. He was convinced that the spot was perfect for his dreams. Nearby Indians were friendly. Rich grasses grew in the area, and the falls of the Spokane River promised waterpower to generate electricity. Glover also believed that a railroad would eventually link Spokane with the country's East Coast and with Puget Sound. He encouraged others to settle nearby.

Even though the railroad took eight years to arrive, Glover's dream came true. In the 1880s, the city became an important rail hub, and the population swelled with 5,000 newcomers each month.

Irrigation channels made it possible to grow fruit on the dry land east of the Cascades.

Life in eastern Washington was even more difficult because of the cold winters and the long distances between homesteads. Wheat farming and cattle ranching were about the only ways to make a living. By 1890, though, ranchers began pumping water from nearby rivers to fields. Called **irrigation,** this process allowed people to grow fruit on the dry grassland.

Most people settled in the Puget Sound region because of the variety of work available. In the years around 1900, Seattle boomed, and ship-building became a major industry.

Washington gained fame as a state where people stood up for what they believed. Workers' organizations such as the Knights of Labor demanded fair wages and safe working conditions. Work in sawmills, for instance, was shortened from 12 to 10 hours a day.

Washington's industries grew even more during the 1940s. The state's many ports made it a good place to build ships and aircraft to send overseas during World War II (1939–1945).

Around this time, the Bonneville Dam, the Grand Coulee Dam, and the Hanford nuclear energy center were constructed. Each of these projects produced enough electricity to run machines in factories. The dams also stored water from the Columbia River to irrigate fields.

Rapid growth in the shipbuilding industry in the early 1900s brought many new jobs to Washington.

Japanese Americans in Washington met with unusual difficulties during World War II. Concerned that they might be spies for Japan, the U.S. government sent thousands of innocent Japanese Americans to prison camps.

The building of the Hanford plant and the two dams brought more jobs and money to the state. This was partly because **hydropower** (electricity generated by water from the dams) was cheap. Thanks to hydropower, factories were built in Washington to make aluminum (a type of metal). In fact, Washington began to produce more aluminum than any other state.

But the changes these projects brought about have not all been positive. For example, since World War II, Hanford has become the most contaminated nuclear site in the United States. Washingtonians are concerned about possible accidents at Hanford that could cause radiation to leak and harm people.

Since World War II, Washington's population has grown rapidly. People have moved to Washington from other states, looking for better jobs and less crowded cities. New industries—including electronics and aerospace—provided jobs for many of these people.

In 1980 Mount Saint Helens erupted, covering parts of Washington with ash and causing floods and forest fires. Fifty-seven people died in the disaster, and plant and animal life was wiped out for miles around.

The construction of the Grand Coulee Dam took eight years, from 1934 to 1942.

Although the eruption of Mount Saint Helens caused terrible destruction, new growth quickly began to bring life back to the area.

By the mid-1990s, the Seattle area was at the center of the world's computer industry. The headquarters of Microsoft Corporation, the world's largest software company, are located in Redmond, near Seattle. Thousands of other computer companies in Washington develop software, design websites, and create new kinds of technology.

Some people have been attracted to Washington by good jobs. Others have come to the state for the beauty of its mountains, water, and forests. As their state becomes more crowded, Washingtonians must learn to balance their state's economic wealth with its natural richness.

Seattle is Washington's largest city. About three out of four Washingtonians live in cities.

PEOPLE & ECONOMY

Scenery, Ships, and Software

By 2000 Washington's fast-growing population had reached about 5.9 million people. Most Washingtonians live in the Puget Sound area, which includes Seattle, Tacoma, and Olympia, the capital. Other major cities include Bellingham in the north, Spokane in the east, and Yakima in central Washington. While the cities have grown quickly over the past few decades, many people have also left. These people have moved to areas such as the San Juan Islands, with their beaches and clean air.

At one time, Native Americans were the only people living in the Pacific Northwest. Modern Washington is home to about 85,000 Indians. This amounts to less than 2 percent of the state's total population. People with European ancestors now make up the majority of Washington's population. About 79 percent of Washingtonians are European Americans.

Other ethnic groups have made their homes in Washington, too. Latinos make up about 8 percent of the population. About 5 percent of Washington's residents are Asian American, and about 3 percent are African American.

Drummers share their art
at a Makah Indian festival.

A Chinese marching team prepares for a colorful parade in Seattle's International District.

Seattle, the state's largest city, has many well-known museums—the Seattle Art Museum, the Pacific Science Center, and the Museum of Flight. The Burke Museum, also in Seattle, and the Museum of Native American Culture in Spokane offer a look into Native American history.

At a county fair in northwestern Washington, a young girl enjoys the farm animals.

People flock to local arts-and-crafts festivals throughout Washington. A town's main street is often blocked to traffic so that craftspeople can display their work. County fairs also are popular summer events, featuring livestock pens and entertainment.

Washington residents and visitors enjoy hiking, fishing, boating, skiing, and camping in the state and national parks. Many Washingtonians like to mountain climb, and Mount Rainier is considered a perfect training ground for beginners and professionals alike. Windsurfers come from all over the world to take advantage of the strong winds in the Columbia Gorge. In professional sports, Washingtonians root for the Super Sonics basketball team, the Mariners baseball team, and the Seahawks football team.

With 29 operating ferries, Washington has the largest ferry system in the United States. Each year, more than 26 million people ride the ferryboats.

Many of the passengers are tourists headed for the San Juan Islands and the Olympic Peninsula. Others are commuters who depend on the ferries to get to and from work in Puget Sound.

More than one out of every eight workers in Washington work in factories that manufacture a variety of products. Many of these people make airplanes, ships, and other transportation equipment. At the Boeing Company, the largest manufacturing employer in the state, thousands of workers produce airplanes and spacecraft. Boeing makes more commercial airplanes than any other company in the country.

From this harbor on Puget Sound, Washingtonians can both admire Mount Rainier and catch a ride on a pleasure boat.

WASHINGTON
Economic Map

The symbols on this map show where different economic activities take place in Washington. The legend below explains what each symbol stands for.

Aircraft	Fruit	Potatoes
Beef cattle/livestock	Grains	Shipbuilding
Computers	Lumber	Tourism
Dairy products	Manufacturing	Vegetables
Fish	Mining	

Asian countries buy much of Washington's lumber, so the wood must be shipped across the Pacific Ocean.

Food processing—the cleaning and canning of fish, berries, and vegetables—is the second most important type of manufacturing. Even salmon eggs, or roe, are carefully packed in salt and shipped to Japan.

Many of Washington's products are shipped across the ocean to Asian countries that line the other side of the Pacific. Washingtonians who work in shipping and trade are called service workers because they perform a service for other businesses.

Other service workers include teachers, bank tellers, and computer software developers. Washington makes more computer software than most other states. About 63 percent of Washington's workers have service jobs.

Washington's Apples

Since the 1920s, Washington has been the number-one producer of apples in the United States. Each year the state's orchards raise more than 100 million bushels of apples (1 bushel equals about 100 apples). Most are Red Delicious apples *(above)*.

When the trees blossom in June, the flowers are thinned by hand. By August the branches need wooden props to keep the weight of the apples from breaking the limbs. When the apples ripen in September, growers depend on thousands of migrant, or traveling, workers to pick the fruit by hand.

The apples are then sorted, packed in boxes, and shipped to cities all over the world. Nearly three-fourths of the apples from Washington are sold as fresh fruit. The rest are processed into juice, jam, and applesauce.

More than one out of every five working Washingtonians are involved in trade. This is partly because Washington is closer to Asia than most other states are. Forest products, cars, chemicals, and foods are some of the products bought and sold.

Seattle is an important **containerport**—one of the largest in the United States. At the port's docks, huge containers—a whole train car or the rear of a truck—arrive full of goods such as electronic equipment, paper products, seafood, and apples. The containers are loaded onto ships that carry the goods across the Pacific Ocean.

In the past, Washington's farmers grew a variety of crops on their land. But modern farms have become more specialized, harvesting only one to three crops. Wheat, potatoes, and apples—all grown in the east—are some of the state's most important crops. Beef cattle graze on eastern ranches, and dairy cows thrive in the west.

A seafood merchant shows his method for making smoked salmon.

Logging is an important industry in western Washington.

For centuries, fishing has provided food for Indians in the Pacific Northwest. When Washington's white settlers began to fish to earn money, the supply of salmon and other fish seemed endless. But by the 1950s, Washingtonians began to realize that they could run out of fish.

Native Americans and white commercial fishers started fighting over who had the right to catch the state's shrinking number of salmon. In 1974 the courts ruled that Indians and whites had equal rights to the salmon. There are still hard feelings between the two fishing groups, but they are working together to leave enough salmon in Washington's waters for future generations.

Logging has played a large part in Washington's history, bringing many people to the state. Some Washingtonians still depend on this industry to make their living. Many of the trees cut each year are ground into pulp, which is then used to make paper products. At lumber mills, logs are cut into boards. Much of Washington's lumber is shipped to Japan.

With its forested mountains and miles of coastline, Washington earns a lot of money from tourists. Service workers help tourists enjoy Washington's state and national parks and other natural areas. They even guide people to Mount Saint Helens. Tourists can view the site of the volcanic eruption from sightseeing helicopters or planes.

Visitors and Washingtonians alike value the state's ocean beaches, thick forests, and rugged mountains. As industries expand and more people move to the state, residents are debating how to protect Washington's beauty and natural resources.

A sunset casts an orange glow over the Washington coast.

THE ENVIRONMENT

Saving the Salmon

Compared to some parts of the United States, Washington seems like a paradise. Mountain wilderness and long, peaceful beaches grace western Washington, while the land and sky stretch endlessly east of the Cascades. Washington's natural beauty attracts tourists and helps create a variety of jobs. Many of the jobs depend on natural resources—trees for lumber, fish for food, and water for irrigation and electricity.

Some residents are concerned that industries are using up Washington's natural resources. Without these resources, many people could lose their jobs.

The future of Washington's fishing villages depends on the future of salmon.

A Chinook salmon swims through a shallow stream.

Other Washingtonians fear for plants and animals when people change the environment. Together, these concerns show that problems faced by plants and animals can signal problems for people, too.

The story of Washington's salmon is a good example of how the lives of people and animals are interconnected. The fish begin their lives in fresh-water streams hundreds of miles from the sea. As the salmon grow up, they swim to the saltwater ocean, where they will spend most of their adult lives. Just before they die, they return to their birth-place to spawn, or lay their eggs.

Salmon and other natural resources were once so plentiful that most people believed they would never run out.

During their long journey to the ocean and back, the fish encounter many dangers. At their spawning grounds, the salmon cannot dig nests unless the water is a certain depth. When loggers cut down trees near rivers, soil slides easily down the bare banks into the water, burying the spawning beds. Bad weather conditions, such as flooding and dry spells, can also change the depth of the water and prevent salmon from spawning.

When the fish do spawn, the baby salmon that hatch and survive swim downstream through farming areas. Farmers often spray their fields with poisonous chemicals to kill insects and make crops grow better. When it rains, the chemicals are washed into rivers, polluting the water and the fish.

Farmers also channel water from rivers to irrigate crops, lowering the water level in the streams. If the salmon live to make it farther downstream, they face hydroelectric dams and polluted waters near towns and cities. Of those salmon that reach the ocean, many are netted by commercial fishers and sold to markets around the world.

When irrigation sprinklers pump water from rivers, salmon streams may become dangerously shallow.

Deadly Dams

Hydroelectric dams, such as Bonneville Dam (above), seriously threaten the lives of salmon. When they head upriver to spawn, the salmon can't jump over the steep cement walls of the dams. Fish ladders (inset) have been added so the salmon can climb the height of the dam one step at a time. But some fish don't find the ladders. Others die at the top because they get confused and lost in the slow-moving water of the reservoir, or artificial lake created by the dam. At each dam, about one out of every ten salmon die.

Heading downriver, the young salmon, called smolts, run into even more problems from dams. The reservoir is warmer than the rest of the river, and some smolts die from overheating or disease.

With so many dams, the journey to the ocean takes much longer than it did before the dams were built. This gives predators such as bears and otters more time to prey on the smolts. The slower journey also means the salmon will not be able to adjust as well to life in salt water when they finally reach the ocean.

The engines that produce electricity at the dams can be deadly, too. Many of the smolts get caught and ground up in the blades of these engines. In all, three-fourths or more of all smolts die on the downriver journey because of dams.

Harm that comes to the salmon also affects other wildlife that depend on salmon. Ducks and trout eat salmon eggs, and bears, otters, and bald eagles eat young salmon. At sea, salmon are food for dolphins, seals, and killer whales. Even plants depend on the nutrients they get from the salmon that die and decay along the mountain streambeds after spawning.

Salmon are strong enough to leap up waterfalls on their journey to spawn. But dams are too high for the fish to leap without help.

The numbers of salmon have dropped so drastically that some species, or types, have been added to the endangered species list. That means they are in danger of becoming extinct, and people must follow guidelines to save the salmon from dying out.

Efforts to save the salmon affect nearly everyone in Washington. Fishers must catch fewer salmon. Farmers must use less water for irrigation. Dams must have fish ladders. Power companies must use less water to create electric power, and customers must pay more for electric power.

Workers at hatcheries in Washington raise thousands of salmon.

Other efforts to increase the numbers of salmon include raising them in hatcheries. But hatchery fish are not as strong as wild fish. They are more likely to catch diseases and do not swim as well in rough water. In addition, when hatchery salmon breed with wild salmon, the weaknesses are passed on to the wild offspring.

For centuries, American Indians honored the salmon like a king. Saving this unique fish from extinction will not be easy. But Washingtonians could pay a much higher price by letting the salmon die out. People in the fishing and seafood-processing industries depend on salmon for their jobs. People who work in coastal towns depend on the money that sport fishers spend on their vacations. And some shipping companies earn money from transporting the salmon to markets.

Washington's waterways and wildlife are precious resources.

Washingtonians will have to continue to work together to preserve the salmon that nourish so many animals, plants, and people throughout the state.

Fun Facts

On May 18, 1980, Washington's Mount Saint Helens erupted for the first time in 123 years, sending a plume of ash 11 miles into the air. The eruption covered some towns with as much as 7 inches of volcanic ash.

Washington is one of the few states where you can see hundreds of nesting bald eagles. This awe-inspiring bird is a threatened species in most of the United States.

Washington is the only state named for a U.S. president. The state takes its name from George Washington, the first president. There's even a city called George, Washington!

George Washington

In Washington some people claim to have seen Sasquatch, or Bigfoot. Legends of this huge, hairy, harmless creature have been passed down since Native Americans first lived in the region. But no one can say for sure if Bigfoot really exists.

As tall as a 46-story building, Grand Coulee Dam on the Columbia River in Washington is the largest concrete structure in the United States. It's also the third largest producer of electricity in the entire world.

Sonora Louise Smart Dodd of Spokane organized the first Father's Day celebration. Inspired by Mother's Day, Dodd wanted a special day to honor her father, William Jackson Smart, and other fathers all over the world. Americans celebrate Father's Day on the third Sunday in June.

STATE SONG

"Washington, My Home" was officially adopted as Washington's state song in 1959. It replaced "Washington Beloved," a popular song that was never officially adopted as the state song.

WASHINGTON, MY HOME

written by Helen Davis, arranged by Stuart Churchill

Wash-ing-ton my home; Where-ev-er I may roam; This is my land, my na-tive land,

Wash-ing-ton, my home. Our ver-dant for-est green, Ca-ressed by sil-v'ry stream. From

moun-tain peak To fields of wheat, Wash-ing-ton, my home. There's peace you feel and un-der-stand In

this, our own be-lov-ed land. We greet the day with head held high, And

for-ward ev-er is our cry, We'll hap-py ev-er be As

peo-ple al-ways free. For you and me a des-tin-y; Wash-ing-ton, my home.

A WASHINGTON RECIPE

Washington produces more apples than any other state. You can make an apple pie with this recipe.

WASHINGTON APPLE PIE

Crust:

Use two pre-made folded pie crusts. You can find these in the refrigerated food section of the supermarket. To prepare the crusts, follow the directions on the package.

Filling:

6 apples (Granny Smiths are especially good)
¼ cup brown sugar
¼ cup white sugar
¼ teaspoon cinnamon

¼ teaspoon nutmeg
1 tablespoon cornstarch
2 tablespoons butter
2 tablespoons orange juice

To make the filling:

1. Have an adult help you peel the apples and remove the cores. Cut into thin slices.
2. In a large bowl, mix the apple slices with the sugars, cinnamon, nutmeg, and cornstarch.

To make the pie:

1. Have an adult preheat the oven to 450° F.
2. Put one of the pie crusts in a 9-inch pie pan.
3. Gently fill the pie shell with the apple mixture. Then sprinkle it with the orange juice.
4. Place the other crust over the top and pinch the top and bottom crust edges together.
5. Prick the top crust with a fork in several places.
6. Bake at 450°F for 10 minutes.
7. Lower the heat to 350°F and bake for 35–45 minutes longer, or until the crust looks done.
8. Cool in pie plate on a wire cooling rack. Serve warm or cold.

HISTORICAL TIMELINE

1500 B.C.   Mount Saint Helens erupts.

A.D. 1500   The Ozette mud slide buries an Indian village.

1700   Indians east of the Cascades begin using horses.

1775   The first Europeans reach the area of Washington.

1792   George Vancouver explores the Pacific Northwest.

1805   Lewis and Clark reach Washington by land.

1825   John McLoughlin builds Fort Vancouver.

1847   Cayuse Indians kill missionaries Marcus and Narcissa Whitman.

1853   Congress creates the Washington Territory.

1883   The completion of the Northern Pacific Railway links Washington and the eastern United States.

1889   Washington becomes the 42nd state.

1896 The discovery of gold in Canada's Yukon Territory leads many new settlers to Washington.

1916 Puget Sound becomes a center for shipbuilding.

1942 The Grand Coulee Dam is completed.

1962 A world's fair called Century 21 is held in Seattle.

1969 Seattle-based Boeing Company oversees the Apollo project that puts the first man on the moon.

1974 Courts rule that white commerical fishers and Native Americans must share salmon fishing rights.

1980 Mount Saint Helens erupts.

1996 Gary Locke becomes the first person of Chinese ancestry to be elected governor of a U.S. state.

1998 The success of the Microsoft Corporation makes chairman Bill Gates the world's richest person.

2001 A strong earthquake strikes the area around Seattle.

OUTSTANDING WASHINGTONIANS

Eddie Bauer

Jeff Bezos

Bing Crosby

Earl Anthony (born 1938) is from Tacoma. As a professional bowler, he won 41 Professional Bowlers Association (PBA) tournaments and is a member of the PBA Hall of Fame.

Eddie Bauer (1899–1986) of Orcas Island, Washington, was the first to make and sell winter coats quilted with goose down. The Eddie Bauer mail-order business, started in 1921, grew to include stores that sell a wide variety of outdoor gear and clothing.

Barbara Helen Berger (born 1945) lives on Bainbridge Island, Washington. A children's illustrator and writer, she has won awards for her books, including *Grandfather Twilight*, *The Donkey's Dream*, and *Gwinna*.

Jeff Bezos (born 1964) moved to Seattle in 1994 and founded Amazon.com, one of the largest Internet-based businesses in the world. Through its sales of books, music, and many other products, Amazon.com has helped introduce people to a new way of shopping. He was named *Time* magazine's 1999 Person of the Year.

Bing Crosby (1904–1977) was born in Tacoma. A popular singer and actor, Crosby starred in more than 50 movies. His recordings of the song "White Christmas" continue to be bestsellers.

John Elway (born 1960) quarterbacked for the Denver Broncos from 1983 to 1998. Elway led his team to the Super Bowl five times, winning twice. Many fans consider him one of the best quarterbacks in football history. Elway is from Port Angeles, Washington.

John Elway

Thomas S. Foley (born 1929) represented Washington in the U.S. House of Representatives from 1965 until 1994. For the last five of those years, the Democrat served as Speaker of the House. He was the U.S. Ambassador to Japan from 1997 until 2001. Foley was born in Spokane.

William Gates III

William Henry Gates III (born 1955) began writing computer programs at the age of 14, before computers were widely used. In 1975 he started the Microsoft Corporation, which makes software for computers. Gates, who is sometimes called the King of Software, is from Seattle.

Richard Gordon Jr.

Richard Gordon Jr. (born 1929) piloted the *Gemini XI* space flight around Earth in 1966. In 1969 the astronaut flew the *Apollo XII* spacecraft for the second landing on the moon. Gordon is from Seattle.

Denis Hayes (born 1944) organized the first Earth Day in 1970 and planned the first international Earth Day in 1990. Earth Day, celebrated yearly on April 22, is a day for people to learn how to keep the earth clean and safe for all living things. Hayes grew up in Camas, Washington.

Denis Hayes

Jimi Hendrix (1942–1970) is considered by some to be the best electric guitarist of all time. During his short career, he led a rock group called the Jimi Hendrix Experience. He also performed solo. Hendrix grew up in Seattle.

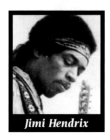

Jimi Hendrix

Frank Herbert (1920–1986) created and wrote about science-fiction worlds in *Dune* and other books. He won several science-fiction awards for his work. Herbert grew up in Tacoma.

Henry Jackson

Henry ("Scoop") Jackson (1912–1983) grew up in Everett and became a U.S. senator in 1953. Jackson supported the rights of minority groups and organized workers' groups. He also helped pass laws to conserve the use of energy.

Robert Joffrey (1930-1988), whose original name was Abdullah Jaffa Bey Khan, was a dancer and choreographer. The Seattle native founded the Joffrey Ballet in New York City in 1956. His dance company is still famous for its combinations of ballet and modern dance.

Chuck Jones

Chuck Jones (born 1912) from Spokane, developed the Looney Tunes and Merrie Melodies cartoons while working at Warner Brothers Pictures. Jones also created the cartoon characters Road Runner, Wile E. Coyote, and Pepe le Pew.

Hank Ketcham (1920–2001) created the comic strip "Dennis the Menace," basing the main character on his son Dennis. Ketcham drew the strip from 1951 to 1994. It still appears in more than 1,000 newspapers worldwide. Ketcham was from Seattle.

Carolyn Kizer

Carolyn Kizer (born 1925) is a poet who was born in Spokane. In 1985 she won the Pulitzer Prize for her collection of poetry called *Yin: New Poems*. Kizer is also the founder and former editor of the magazine *Poetry Northwest*.

Gary Larson

Gary Larson (born 1950) of Tacoma, Washington, created the comic strip "The Far Side." Although Larson retired in 1995, his cartoons remain popular for their unusual brand of humor.

Chief Seattle (1786?–1866), a wise and respected leader, was born on Puget Sound to a Duwamish mother and a Suquamish father. In his most famous speech, given in 1854, Seattle noted how quickly the land that the Indians had held for thousands of years would pass to white settlers.

Chief Seattle

Robert Franklin Stroud (1890–1963) of Seattle became known as the Bird-Man of Alcatraz. Stroud spent part of his 55-year prison term in Alcatraz, a former California prison. While serving his sentence, Stroud studied and cared for birds, becoming an expert in the field. He also earned college degrees in five different subjects.

Robert Stroud

George Tsutakawa (1910–1997) grew up in Seattle and became a well-known sculptor. Some of his most famous sculptures are bronze fountains in parks in the United States and in Japan.

Adam West (born 1938) played the role of Batman in the 1966 film *Batman* and in the popular 1960s television series of the same name. West is from Walla Walla, Washington.

Adam West

James Whittaker (born 1929) was the first U.S. athlete to successfully climb Asia's Mount Everest, the world's highest peak. He has also reached the top of Washington's Mount Rainier 66 times. Whittaker is from Port Townsend, Washington.

Minoru Yamasaki (1912–1986) was an architect from Seattle who designed more than 300 buildings. His most famous building is probably the World Trade Center in New York City.

Minoru Yamasaki

FACTS-AT-A-GLANCE

Nickname: Evergreen State

Song: "Washington, My Home"

Motto: Alki (an Indian word for "By and By")

Flower: coast rhododendron

Tree: western hemlock

Bird: willow goldfinch

Fish: steelhead trout

Insect: green darner dragonfly

Fossil: Columbian mammoth

Date and ranking of statehood:
November 11, 1889, the 42nd state

Capital: Olympia

Area: 66,581 square miles

Rank in area, nationwide: 20th

Average January temperature: 30° F

Average July temperature: 66° F

Washington's state flag features George Washington, the president for whom the state was named. The green background represents the nickname "Evergreen State."

POPULATION GROWTH

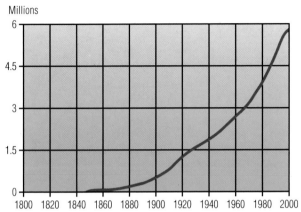

Millions

This chart shows how Washington's population has grown from 1850 to 2000.

A jeweler from Olympia, Charles Talcott, designed Washington's state seal in 1889. His brother George found the model for the picture of George Washington— on a box of cold medicine. An updated design was adopted in 1967.

Population: 5,894,121 (2000 Census)

Rank in population, nationwide: 15th

Major cities and populations: (2000 Census) Seattle (563,374), Spokane (195,629), Tacoma (193,556), Vancouver (143,560), Bellevue (109,569), Everett (91,488)

U.S. senators: 2

U.S. representatives: 9

Electoral votes: 11

Natural resources: clay, coal, fish, forests, gold, gravel, lead, limestone, sand, seafood, soil, water, zinc

Agricultural products: apples, beef, cherries, dairy products, flower bulbs, grapes, plums, potatoes, wheat

Fishing industry: cod, crabs, flounder, halibut, herring, oysters, rockfish, salmon, shrimp, steelhead, tuna

Manufactured goods: airplanes, chemicals, computer software, doors, food products, lumber, paper, plywood, shipping containers, ships, spacecraft, wood chips

WHERE WASHINGTONIANS WORK

Services—63 percent (services include jobs in trade; community, social, and personal services; finance, insurance, and real estate; transportation, communication, and utilities)

Government—16 percent

Manufacturing—12 percent

Construction—5 percent

Agriculture—4 percent

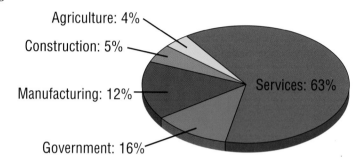

Agriculture: 4%
Construction: 5%
Manufacturing: 12%
Government: 16%
Services: 63%

GROSS STATE PRODUCT

Services—64 percent

Government—15 percent

Manufacturing—13 percent

Construction—5 percent

Agriculture—3 percent

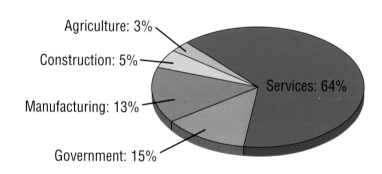

Agriculture: 3%
Construction: 5%
Manufacturing: 13%
Government: 15%
Services: 64%

WASHINGTON WILDLIFE

Mammals: beaver, black bear, gray whale, mountain goat, mule deer, orca

Birds: bald eagle, great blue heron, northern spotted owl, Stellar's jay

Reptiles and amphibians: common garter snake, Pacific gopher snake, painted turtle, western skink

Fish: albacore tuna, cod, salmon, sturgeon, trout, whitefish

Trees: Douglas fir, pine, western hemlock, western larch

Wild plants: fern, goldenrod, lupine, sagebrush, wild onion

A deer crosses a stream near the Cascade River.

PLACES TO VISIT

Boeing Tour Center, Everett
At Boeing's 11-story assembly plant, visitors can get an up-close look at how airplanes are built.

Capitol Campus, Olympia
One of the most beautiful state capitols in the United States, the Capitol Campus includes an arboretum, a rose garden, and a 287-foot dome—the fifth largest in the world.

Fort Vancouver National Historic Site, Vancouver
Once a British trading center, the fort features many restored buildings. Guided tours include a look at a working blacksmith's forge.

Makah Cultural and Research Center, Neah Bay
Located on the Makah Indian Reservation in the northwest corner of Washington, this museum contains artifacts preserved by the Ozette mud slide.

Mount Saint Helens National Volcanic Monument
The grounds surrounding the famous volcano include places to hike and camp, as well as several visitor centers devoted to sharing the story of the 1980 eruption.

Olympic National Park
Located in the heart of the Olympic Mountains in the northern Coast Ranges, the park is an excellent place to visit rain forests and see Washington's wildlife.

Palouse Falls State Park

This southeastern park is the home of one of the most amazing waterfalls in Washington. On sunny days, the spray from the 200-foot plunge often creates rainbows.

Rocky Reach Dam, near Wenatchee

Spanning the Columbia River, the dam features a huge museum and a fish viewing room where salmon are visible from April through November.

San Juan Islands

Just a ferry ride away from the mainland city of Anacortes, the islands are wonderful places for biking, boating, camping, and whale watching.

Seattle Center

This area was the site of Century 21, a world's fair held in 1962. The towering Space Needle, the Pacific Science Center, and the Children's Museum are all located here, along with an amusement park.

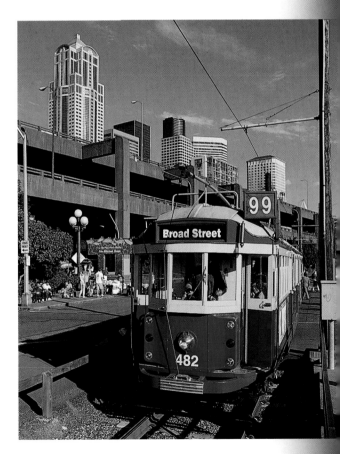

Streetcars travel along Seattle's waterfront.

ANNUAL EVENTS

Seagull Calling Festival, Port Orchard—*April*

Skagit Valley Tulip Festival, Skagit County—*April*

Bloomsday Run, Spokane—*May*

Juan de Fuca Art Festival, Port Angeles—*May*

Toppenish Indian Pow Wow, Toppenish—*July*

Washington State International Kite Festival, Long Beach—*August*

Alternative Fuel Fair and Electric Car Races, Lacey—*September*

Wenatchee River Salmon Festival, Leavenworth—*September*

Wooden Boat Festival, Port Townsend—*September*

Issaquah Salmon Days Festival, Issaquah—*October*

LEARN MORE ABOUT WASHINGTON

BOOKS

General

Fradin, Dennis B., and Judith Bloom Fradin. *Washington.* Danbury, CT: Children's Press, 1997.

Stefoff, Rebecca. *Washington.* New York: Benchmark Books, 1999. For older readers.

Special Interest

Charnan, Simon. *Bill Gates: Helping People Use Computers.* New York: Children's Press, 1997. A biography of the billionaire who founded Microsoft Corporation and has influenced the way computers are used all over the world.

Hirschi, Ron. *Salmon.* Minneapolis: Carolrhoda Books, 2001. Hirschi details the salmon's natural history, life cycle, and struggle to survive in modern North America. Illustrated with color photographs.

Lauber, Patricia. *Volcano: The Eruption and Healing of Mount St. Helens.* New York: Aladdin Books, 1993. This photo essay, a Newbery Honor Book, features a detailed look at the 1980 eruption of Mount Saint Helens and the gradual return of wildlife to the area. Includes color photographs.

Savage, Jeff. *Drew Bledsoe: Cool Quarterback*. Minneapolis: Lerner Publications Company, 1999. A biography of the football star, who was born in Ellensburg, Washington.

Wright-Frierson, Virginia. *A North American Rainforest Scrapbook*. New York: Walker & Co., 1999. A nature artist guides readers on a hike through the rain forest of Washington's Olympic Peninsula. The area's plants and animals are illustrated with watercolor paintings.

Fiction

Hamm, Diane Johnston. *Daughter of Suqua*. Morton Grove, IL: Albert Whitman, 1997. Ida, a ten-year-old Suquamish girl, lives in a village on Puget Sound in the early 1900s, a time when her people are losing their land to the U.S. government.

Holm, Jennifer L. *Our Only May Amelia*. New York: HarperCollins, 1999. Set in Washington in 1899, this Newbery Honor Book tells the story of 12-year-old May Amelia. The only girl in a Finnish immigrant family of eight children, May Amelia refuses to behave like a "Proper Young Lady" and encounters plenty of trouble as a result.

WEBSITES

Access Washington Home Page
<http://www.access.wa.gov/>
Washington's official website includes government news, facts about state services, and a list of great sites for kids.

Official Washington State Tourism Website
<http://www.experiencewashington.com>
For up-to-date information about everything from Washington festivals to weather, visit this website.

The Seattle Times
<http://www.seattletimes.nwsource.com>
Read about current events in the online version of this popular Washington newspaper.

Seattle Art Museum
<http://www.seattleartmuseum.org/>
Learn about art in Washington and around the world, view online exhibits, and check out the section for kids.

Washington Apple Commission
<http://www.bestapples.com/>
The online tribute to this important crop features recipes, apple facts, and an Apple Guy who can answer questions by e-mail.

PRONUNCIATION GUIDE

Cayuse (KY-yoos)

Chelan (shuh-LAN)

Chinook (shuh-NOOK)

Juan de Fuca (wahn duh FYOO-kuh)

Makah (mah-KAW)

Nez Percé (NEZ PURS)

Palouse (puh-LOOS)

Puget Sound (PYOO-juht sownd)

Rainier (ruh-NIHR)

Seattle (see-AT-uhl)

Spokane (spok-KAN)

Tacoma (tuh-KOH-muh)

Vancouver (van-KOO-vur)

Yakima (YAK-uh-maw)

Hiking is a popular activity in Washington's rocky foothills.

GLOSSARY

containerport: shipping port that is specially designed to handle cargo packed in large containers, such as train cars

glacier: large body of ice and snow that moves slowly over land

hydropower: electricity produced by the force of flowing water; also called hydroelectric power

irrigation: method of watering land by directing water through canals, ditches, pipes, or sprinklers

missionary: person sent out by a religious group to spread its beliefs to other people

plateau: large, relatively flat area that stands above the surrounding land

rain forest: thick, wet, evergreen forest with an annual rainfall of more than 100 inches. Most rain forests are located in hot, wet climates near the equator. Washington has one of the few rain forests found in cooler climates.

reservation: public land set aside by the government to be used by Native Americans

scabland: rocky land that was stripped of its soil when floods from melting glaciers washed away the soil

strait: narrow stretch of water that connects two larger bodies of water

treaty: agreement between two or more groups, usually having to do with peace or trade

INDEX

PHOTO ACKNOWLEDGMENTS

Cover photographs by ©Neil Rabinowitz/CORBIS (left), and ©Philip James Corwin/CORBIS (right). ©Wolfgang Kaehler, pp. 2-3, 3, 4 (detail), 6, 7 (detail), 19 (detail), 41 (detail), 52 (detail), 59, 75; LINK/Visuals Unlimited, p. 7; PresentationMaps.com, pp. 1, 8, 9, 46; Tore Ofteness, pp. 11, 12, 14 (left), 15, 20, 51, 55; Jon Brunk, pp. 13, 44, 45, 47, 49, 52; Patrick Cone, p. 14 (right); ©Karen Huntt Mason/CORBIS, p. 16; Jay A. Beck, p. 17; Diane Cooper, p. 18 (both); Burke Museum (#25.0/145), p. 19; Special Collections Div., Univ. of Washington Libraries, pp. 21, 54, 69 (top) (Curtis #34127); ©Richard A. Cooke/CORBIS, p. 22; Museum of History and Industry, pp. 23, 32, 33, 35, 36, 37; Library of Congress, pp. 24, 38; Kay Shaw, p. 26; Bryan Peterson, Legislative Media Services, p. 27; Oregon Historical Society (neg. #803), p. 28; National Park Service, p. 29 (both); Washington State Historical Society, Tacoma, p. 31; Eastern Washington State Historical Society, p. 34 (both); ©Layne Kennedy/CORBIS, p. 39; ©Philip James/CORBIS, pp. 40, 56; Jens Lund/Washington State Folklife Council, p. 42; Jim Corwin/Allstock, p. 43; Patricia Drentea, p. 48; Root Resources, p. 50; Oregon Department of Fish and Wildlife, p. 53; ©William J. Weber, p. 56 (inset); U.S. Dept. of Fish and Wildlife, Marvina Munch, p. 57; Ruth A. Smith/Root Resouces, p. 58; Pennsylvania Academy of the Fine Arts, p. 60; Toby Schnobrich, p. 61; Tim Seeley, pp. 63, 71, 72; Eddie Bauer, Outdoor Outfitter, p. 66 (top); ©Reuters NewMedia Inc./CORBIS, pp. 66 (second from top), 67 (top); TV Times, p. 66 (second from bottom); Independent Picture Service, p. 66 (bottom); NASA, p. 67 (second from top); Tony Russo, p. 67 (second from bottom); Reprise Records, p. 67 (bottom); ©Bettmann/CORBIS, pp. 68 (top, second from top); Carolyn Kizer, p. 68 (second from bottom); Universal Press Syndicate, p. 68 (bottom); National Archives, p. 69 (second from top); Hollywood Book & Poster, Inc., p. 69 (second from bottom); Taro Yamasaki/Daniel Bartush, p. 69 (bottom); Jean Matheny, p. 70; ©Joel W. Rogers/CORBIS, p. 73; Byron Crader/Root Resouces, p. 80.